AF256187

THE RAGING LION

THE RAGING LION
The Warrior Mind and Competitive Sports

For my Brother, Randy

"You will never do anything
in this world without
courage. It is the greatest
quality of the mind next to
honor."

James Allen

The Raging Lion
Clifford Beck©2010
Cover Design by Clifford Beck

Table of Contents

The Howling

An oppressive night
a moon on the rise.
A chilly mist hangs
in the air.

A kilted to figure –
vanguard of the dawn
with sword unsheathed.
The blood of his enemy
spattered 'cross his face.

Glory is but a thing of the
moment, whilst honor
goes on for a lifetime.
The fever of battle.
a fire in his eyes.

A Piper's ghost fills the air
with slow, chaotic melodies.
A rumble of thunder,
a flash of celestial light.
A battle cry screams
across the moors.

Preface

In any competitive sport, be it basketball, football, hockey, the SCA, or fencing, there is one element that they all have in common: the need for a warrior mentality. This mindset should not be perceived as a need for aggression, violence, or hostility. On the contrary, the warrior mindset demands a sense of honor, fair play, emotional self-control, and rational thinking, as well as physical strength and endurance.

As for blood sports, the warrior mentality should never tolerate the intentional spilling of blood or rendering of injury. Yes, accidents and injuries do occur in the arena of competition. One does not participate in these activities without accepting this risk. Yet, there is nothing to be gained -- no true respect to be earned – by the purposeful injuring of one's opponent, nor in the celebration of their injuries.

As for the concept of honor, I have come to see honor from more than one perspective. First and foremost, the concept of honor is largely defined within a cultural framework. Every culture holds its own set of ideas regarding what is honorable. This can largely be attributed to such elements as cultural history, language, and social morals. This would also apply to the subject of ethics, as the concepts of honor and ethics are often intertwined.

However, it would seem reasonable to believe that at its core, there would exist a common element on which all cultural ideas of honor or based. One might suggest that honor is based on the concept of right and wrong. Yes, even this idea is largely interpreted by culture. Perhaps what defines honor, at its deepest level, is its opposite – shame -- to bring shame onto oneself, one's family, or in some cultures -- one's community.

Shame, it seems, can be experienced through dishonest, criminal, or offensive acts, with the maintaining of a set of ethics that exists in contradiction to what is acceptable in a given culture. For example, in a country where military service is compulsory, refusing to enlist would be considered a violation of their cultural ethics. This could also possibly be seen as an act of cowardice, and therefore a dishonor, by virtue of the shame it brings.

The perspective of this book is from two separate but closely tied ideas: honor and fair play. Certainly one cannot possess one trait without being in possession of the other. Indeed, they are nearly identical to each other in that both require a certain code of conduct and ethics that presents competition and the competitor in the brightest possible light.

It does not matter if one works within the walls of a cubicle or is a student attending a military academy. The warrior mindset that has been handed down over centuries via the world's many cultures and civilizations will always be relevant. Indeed, regardless of the life one leads, a warrior mentality will foster a sense of ethics, strength of character, and a knowing of oneself that can never be extinguished. In its entirety, this is the fire within that drives us forward -- demanding success, achievement, and victory -- to continue the fight, even when all seems lost. At the same time, never straying from what is correct, ethical, and honorable.

In this work, I will touch upon several schools of thought regarding warfare as it applies to the individual competitor. These philosophies -- both Eastern and Western -- would include the writings of Sun Tzu, The Bushido, as well as the ideas behind the war philosophy of the United States Marine Corps. I will quote ancient, as well as contemporary texts and present commentaries on each while maintaining a perspective consistent with competitive sports. Some degree of original content will also be found here. These sections have been written as additions to describe character traits consistent with the development of the warrior mindset. Additionally, these additions grew out of the flow of creative energy that developed during the research phase of this writing.

Part One
Attitude

To truly earn the respect of one's peers, therefore furthering the development of one's honor, the proper attitude is vital. One can take some degree of pride in one's individuality, but too much of this can be consuming, leading to self-obsession and arrogance. This form of pride is a disease of the self, forcing one way from any further growth or learning. As a result, any new techniques or tactics may be met with resistance, as if to say, 'I know all I need to know'. This is poison to the competitor who believes themselves to be better than all others in their sport, and perhaps others in general.

The reality behind this veil of self-aggrandizement is that there will always be another who will challenge your skills – who will not back down, or be swayed by fear -- someone who is well underway on the warrior's path. Even a person of lesser skill can achieve victory over one is plagued by arrogance, as this attitude has a tendency to occupy so much of their attention that there is little room for anything else.

Call it arrogance, narcissism, or condescension, this attitude can have many names and none of them cast a flattering light on one's character. It holds one back from their true potential, scarring their character and destroying their reputation -- replacing respect with the growing resentment of others.

Occasionally, one can rise above this attitude and earn back their honor, so that others may come to respect and trust them. This, however, does not come without the harsh lesson that one becomes faced with -- that this individual eventually suffers a bone-jarring fall back into the world of humanity. They may begin to experience defeat at the hands of opponents of somewhat lesser skill, but who have learned some of the warrior's ways -- including some degree of humility. Or they may experience some tragic event that pushes them to realize who they are. Only then, regardless of the circumstances that led them there, can they be brought to the beginning of the warrior's path.

Pain and exhaustion

Pain is our closest ally. Exhaustion, however, is the enemy. Pain lets us know when we are injured or ill. It says to us, 'Stop! Something's wrong!' To ignore pain is to invite disaster at the hands of its disabling grip. In competition, it generally demands a withdrawal from the scene, as well as medical attention.

The real enemy that everyone will confront in the competitive arena is exhaustion. It saps one's will, alertness, strength, and determination. If you cannot achieve victory over exhaustion, you will be defeated in the end. There are two approaches to be taken when dealing with this and both must be addressed. The first is, of course, endurance training. This is best accomplished through discipline, as well as a change in one's mental state.

One must bring oneself to begin this training in whatever form is most appropriate -- nothing ever gets accomplished on its own. In the matter of one's mental state, endurance training should be difficult to be effective. Yet, to maintain a degree of rhythm within training, one should perceive training as an act of meditation, training the body and the mind -- both with the same goal of increasing endurance and combating exhaustion.

Key to understanding a training program of any type is to not think about the stress you're putting your body through. Focus on the spot in front of yourself and allow yourself to slip into that moment -- releasing your mind away from the body, and that's the sense of exhaustion. This will allow your mind to stop consciously thinking about what your body is doing, as it already knows what to do.

Courage

War and bloodlust are not to be glorified, as they tend to leave deep, lasting scars on the face of human history. It is the character and courage of the individual warrior that should be commended -- the lone soldier who places himself in the mouth of the beast and defends their country and way of life. Even for the sake of the political machine, it is the warrior that takes up arms without questioning the authority that places him in the theater of battle.

It is courage and bravery that rise into immortality, risking one's very life for the sake of duty. And the epic writings of Homer, the Viking sagas, and the war poems of old still ring with the eternal toll of stories of bravery and courage in the face of certain death.

To face down adversity or impending defeat with character and courage, even when all hope seems lost, is the highest quality of the warrior. To stand fast in the face of the coming storm and continue the fight when defeat is imminent. In the arena of competition, it is this quality we seek. And it is this quality that brings out the best in us -- this never giving up.

For bravery and courage are not self-serving qualities, acting as an empty display of machismo. They are, in fact, expressions of deep perseverance that humanity itself holds at its foundation. This of course, does not mean that people, in general, are prone to acting with courage. Once courage is sought for, it can be discovered and brought to a state of action.

It is only when this is accomplished that we are in possession of what is required to do the impossible. For there are no heroes in this world, merely those who have challenged themselves to do heroic things. Even though they may battle the demon of fear as well, they do not stop, nor do they weaken. It is this

and more that lay at the core of the
warrior soul.

31

Discipline

One may read every ancient and contemporary text ever written on the subject of discipline. But, none will be of any use without a strong sense of commitment. Discipline, in any definition of the word, cannot develop without it. Commitment and discipline know no middle ground and the idea of compromise simply does not exist. One may say that commitment represents the strong, perfectionistic will within the characteristic of discipline.

Commitment requires both a conscious, deliberate decision to succeed and determination to see it through. Discipline, on the other hand, demands work and a single-minded perseverance, to be carried out at the expense of all else.

Some individuals involve themselves in spiritual matters, i.e. Buddhism, yoga, Hindu rituals, and the like, who spend a lifetime learning and building upon their self-discipline. Some might refer to this as 'self-mastery'. This could be seen as the highest form of self-discipline and serves as an example of how far one is willing to go in the commitment to achieve their goals. This by no means should imply that everyone, regardless of their sport, should spend their lives in the mountains of Tibet clad in robes and fingering through a string of prayer beads.

However, the principle is the same. Commitment is absolute and discipline will always demand more than what you possess. But, it is here that one realizes their limitations and works that much harder to surpass them. And, in doing so achieves not only success, but a degree of personal growth and inner strength, which is far more important than success alone.

Emotional Responses

The principle emotion that is usually at work here is anger. In Eastern martial arts, a technique referred to as 'controlled rage' is taught. This is not a true emotional response, but a redirection of primal energy designed to startle an adversary long enough to create a window of opportunity in which to gain an advantage. However, this controlled rage is not appropriate for every competitive sport and is the result of centuries of tradition.

Anger, however, is an unproductive emotion. It robs one of the ability to exercise judgment, concentration, and strategic thinking. This occurs because anger is often all-consuming. After all, we are an aggressive species and anger comes to us with far too much ease. Replacing anger with calm and clarity is only possible with intense training and a drive to outwit one's opponent.

Fear

Fear is an intimate part of who we are as members of humanity. In situations of conflict, fear raises its head with amazing suddenness and is the warrior's greatest foe. It is the beast within that will not be tamed. Like anger, fear robs us of our ability to concentrate. Fear can often be all-consuming, causing us to panic, freeze or hesitate at a critical moment when victory may well be within reach.

In ordinary life, fear can be a valuable asset, letting us know when we are in jeopardy. But in the field of competition, there is little to no room for error or indecision, fear becomes the menace of the moment.

So how do we slay this beast? I believe the best way to approach this is by analogy. Fear, like any other emotion, presents itself as being somewhat irrational. One could see fear as a momentary gust of wind, pushing down a tree or simply blowing through its leaves. However, by merely blowing through the leaves, the tree remains largely unaffected. In a similar manner, fear becomes something that can cause one to topple. Or, it can be nothing more than a momentary internal event that passes through us as leaves on a tree, leaving us unmoved. With a bit of visual imagery, one can easily see the aforementioned analogy as a mental exercise that requires only focus, as well as a strong sense of determination to make it work.

This should not be perceived as the elimination of fear but as a means of coping with it in order to present a show of strength. Outside the arena of competition, this technique can also be used to maintain one's focus in a critical moment and to establish the presentation of inner strength.

Honesty

This can be a difficult subject to approach without accidentally becoming 'preachy', or taking the position of finger-pointing. That being said, honesty can be defined as 'bearing witness to one's actions'. Respect and honesty are deeply intertwined and both can be thought of as possessing equal value within the character of the individual. Should one choose to abandon their honesty, they will lose both their self-respect, as well as the respect of their peers and thus, their honor. These are the consequences of dishonesty and it is dishonesty that flies in opposition to warrior values.

Let us further explore this idea by example: you are a Private First Class in the United States Marine Corps in your battalion has been deployed to an undisclosed area of the Middle East. As a Marine and your fellow Marines have learned a certain code of honor. And yet, when you catch your closest comrade in an obvious act of dishonesty, you begin to question his integrity, motives, and his commitment to the idea of Marines as brothers. You're also forced into questioning not only your choice of friends but also something much more critical. Can this person not be trusted to back me up in a firefight, when all our lives are at stake or when facing almost certain death?

Most of the time, the consequences of dishonesty do not result in such dire circumstances. However, the principles at work here are consistent with any other situation in which respect and trust are lost through an act of dishonesty. The warrior mentality cannot tolerate dishonesty of any kind. In fact, many such cultures consider any act of dishonesty to be equal to an act of cowardice. This would bring shame upon the individual and possibly their family as well.

Be it a cohesive unit bound by the ideas of battle and almost certain death, or a team deployed on the gridiron or soccer field, trust and respect are both important elements to making that unit or team function as one, well-oiled machine. Any deviation from this cohesion, through the loss of trust and respect, will most certainly result in chaos and disintegration of the team. And thus, any hope of achieving victory is now in doubt. Therefore, the cohesion and success of the group rests on the integrity of each member of that group.

The Inexperienced Opponent

The beginning of becoming a warrior in any competitive sport starts with the learning process. Everyone takes that first step on the path of knowledge and training within their chosen sport. All of us start as students. So, should one who is thoroughly trained and experienced go up against those who are just beginning their journey into competition? The answer is certainly yes. However, after one has gained enough knowledge and training in one's chosen sport, there is an application to be met. This is in the role of the teacher.

This role is of great value to the experienced and inexperienced alike, in that those lacking experience, judgment, and wisdom should be received by the tutelage of one who is far more skilled. Conversely, the teacher gains the respect and trust of the student, as well as the wisdom and patience that arise from the very act of teaching the less skilled.

This brings us back to the beginning of this section. Yes, everyone wants to win. Everyone is, at some point, exposed to the sweet taste of victory. But there is absolutely nothing to be gained by an overwhelmed and inexperienced opponent. This fact does in no way constitute a victory. It is shallow, and weak and reveals an individual whose soul has been stained by arrogance and cowardice. This most certainly will result in a loss of respect for one's peers, who will no doubt see them as overbearing and lacking consideration for those of lesser skill. This is the loss of honor. And honor is never bestowed upon -- it can only be lost. This strays far from the warrior's path.

The inexperienced are not preparing themselves to become fodder for the taunting stings and humiliation by those lacking in character and courage. They are learning. A warrior who feels joy and pride and shaming the student, believing it to be a legitimate victory, is no warrior at all. Until one acquires a sense of humility they will not earn the respect of others, or be looked up to by other students. Unless this goal is achieved, they are nothing and do not deserve so much as a passing glance from their peers.

Revenge

In the play 'Hamlet' Shakespeare wrote, "Revenge is a dish best served cold". While this statement is open to interpretation, is the idea of revenge that we shall touch upon here. Throughout history there has been, and continues to be, a great deal of violence and bloodshed committed in the name of revenge. From the clan warfare of northern Europe to gang violence on the streets of Los Angeles, human history is filled with violent acts of vengeance.

The true warrior must be immune from carrying out any act of revenge if he/she is to continue receiving the respect of their peers. Thus, maintaining a sense of honor and bringing a degree of dignity to their conduct, as well as their sport. At the same time, there is one particular aspect of this issue that is acceptable, but only if it is acted upon with great care. The idea of success as revenge is rarely considered in general, as we are all aggressive by virtue of human nature.

Success is the best form of revenge and must be accomplished as a legitimate act. And after this is successfully achieved, it must also be met with dignity. Such things as taunting or harassing the opponent you have just defeated by neither honorable nor are they respectful toward your opponent. In fact, this type of behavior often provokes an unwanted and sometimes violent response. And in some combat sports, taunting one's opponent can often result in a penalty or even being ejected from competition.

While many may agree that those who are prone to cheating, confrontational behavior, or conduct meant to demean others should be put in their place, it is important to realize that revenge only acts to bring us down to their level. We, in turn, lose the respect of our peers, as well as our honor. But, success as revenge is a different sort of beast determined not to slide into those aggressive actions or attitudes that we may rise above them.

Strategic vs. Tactical Thinking

Many people use the phrases 'strategic thinking' and 'tactical thinking' interchangeably. In actuality, these ideas are very different from each other, yet they are very closely tied together. The American Heritage Dictionary provides a precise definition of each term, but I will discuss them here by example.

Let us first examine these ideas from a military perspective. 'Strategy' is thought of as the planning phase involved in the execution of combat operations, regardless of its scale. 'Tactics' refers to the resources, techniques, and deployment of troops against the enemy.

So, how do these concepts translate to competitive sports? As far as team sports are concerned, football would be a good example. Strategy is often dictated by existing playbooks, while tactics becomes more a quality of what the players bring to the game – their physical condition, endurance, speed, and the ability to think quickly under pressure, as well as positions for which they are trained. The team sports such as this most closely resembles the military model, from a command structure to the deployment and maneuvering of ground forces.

But what of combat sports -- Greco-Roman wrestling, fencing, or the Eastern martial arts? Most definitely, strategy and tactics hold an important place in these sports as well, where planning and execution exist for the sake of victory. These sports are based largely on age-old techniques and proper form. These elements can be taken collectively as the source of strategy, as well as a system of tactical maneuvers. For example, in the martial arts, there is a form of training called 'Kata', which consists of a prescribed set of techniques used to fight an imaginary attacker. One could think of these forms as the dictionary of the martial arts and the basis of strategy. And yet, when techniques are separated from the forms, they become the source of tactics.

Whether the goal is to pin an opponent, land a touch, score a touchdown, or execute a solid kick, planning one's attack must always be followed by the pooling together of one's resources in order to make that plan work successfully.

Part Two

Commentary on
The Hagakure

"If you gaze at a single leaf on a tree, you do not see the other leaves. If you face the tree with no intention and don't fix your eyes on a single leaf, then you see all the many leaves."

How important is it to see? After all, we do it all the time -- we look at this, glance at that. We can even imagine an image in our minds. But, for the warrior -- competitor, there is a clear and crucial difference between seeing and looking.

Looking at one thing can often distract us from the larger picture. For example, focusing on your opponent's eyes. Human nature and social etiquette often demand by contact enemy engage in this on an unconscious level. However, as a target, the eyes are very small in relation to the rest of the body. And focusing on another part of the body, such as the hands, provides just as much a distraction as eye contact. But what is the difference between seeing and looking? And what does it mean to 'see'? 'Looking' may imply consciously focusing on an object, while 'seeing' can be thought of as a perception of the whole body. If this sort of perception can be learned, you will begin to see the whole of your opponent. When they move, do not allow this perception to alter, but continue to look through your opponent -- seeing the whole. As you continue with this new perception, you will begin to see movement in your opponent without focusing on that movement.

How do we achieve this new perception? Clearly, there is no shortcut, no timesaving secret technique involved. To master this requires practice and with any object -- a house, a tree, a painting, or sculpture. You must discard your first instinct to look at every detail and allow yourself to see past the object.

Practicing this can soon come to feel like a state of meditation -- the act of focusing on nothing and yet being able to see everything. Admittedly, this seems somewhat esoteric, yet its application is quite practical. If you come to see everything of your opponent without attending to any one specific detail, it then becomes easier to see any slight movement and react accordingly. This will give you the advantage of seeing all the details at once, without the anxiety of trying to predict what your opponent will do next. You'll perceive their movement before they realize that they have done anything.

"If one thinks only of winning, sordid victory will be worse than defeat."

Winning at any cost is unacceptable to the warrior -- competitor who insists on maintaining their honor through honesty. Taking advantage of a loophole in the rules of a given sport may be technically correct, but it is hardly the correct action of one who wishes to continue receiving the respect of his peers. An honest victory is a legitimate victory and one should never resort to bending, or otherwise exploiting the rules of the game in order to compensate for a lack of skill. The adage "It's not whether you win or lose, but how you play the game", certainly applies here. And, one cannot achieve it occurs under a cloud of doubt and suspicion.

Should one suffer defeat at the hands of a competent opponent, they can still walk away with their honor and self-respect intact. However, winning by manipulation of the rules is a hollow victory at best. It leads to the respect and trust given by one's peers to become tainted and replaced by the glancing eye of suspicion.

"When meeting with difficult situations, one should -- forward bravely and with joy."

The world is a cold, cruel, and unfair place where nothing is ever as simple or as easy as we believe it should be. It is a place where success is achieved with difficulty failure comes at a price. The point is, that anything worth doing will be difficult, and victory that is accomplished through training and hard work will be that much sweeter.

Life is also filled with compromise. However, where success and hard work are involved, there should be not a whisper of compromise. Set your goals. Dream your dreams. Attack your life on hands and knees, crawling through whatever the world throws at you.

Even if no one shows appreciation for your efforts, you will have better yourself. In the end, your victory requires the approval of no one and you will be the only person you need to impress.

"Do not rely upon following a degree of understanding that you have discovered, but simply think, 'This is not enough'."

It is important to have faith in one's training and skills. This is called confidence. However, when we stop learning, defeat will surely come knocking. Therefore, our abilities become limited by our resistance to the learning process. Certainly, we cannot know everything -- the universe is simply too vast and we are too small. And yet, there is so much more one can learn. It is with this perspective in mind that we may learn and grow, untethered by the restraints of ego. But only if we are willing to make the journey, as the open and willing mind can never learn enough. It becomes a sponge cast into an ocean of knowledge, absorbing as much as possible and using what he learns as the moment necessitates it.

The warrior is one who refuses to stop learning. And, as you walk the path of your particular art, you must realize that this path never ends. The act of learning within the arena of competition is accomplished for its own sake. This can also be seen in the manner in which one lives life in general. Knowledge is everywhere. And with knowledge comes the increasing ability to plan, to think ahead of your opponent, and continue to build confidence in your skills.

Commentary on Sun Tzu

"Thus one who is skillful at keeping the enemy on the move maintains deceitful appearances, according to which the enemy will act."

The possibility of invasion as a defense exists in almost all competitive sports. Keeping your opponent at bay is key to successfully evading any strategy to gain the upper hand. But why would this be necessary? Let us consider, for example, a martial arts tournament. A bout is three minutes long and you have a one-point lead of 4 to 3. At this point, time can become your ally. Now you're in a position to determine the outcome without scoring the additional point.

If you can keep your opponent moving through evasive tactics, then you have forced the element of time into the role of ally. As time runs out, your opponent may begin to reject out of desperation, driven to score a point that will tie the bout. But since you have the upper hand already, you can maintain this by evasion and allow you to expend the remaining bout time and achieve victory.

"Let your plans the dark and impenetrable as night, and when you move, fall like a thunderbolt."

This idea can best be approached through the concept of body language. The ancient Greeks taught in philosophy called 'dualism', which teaches that the mind and body are intimately intertwined. What affects the mind can be expressed through the body and what impacts the body can be reflected in the mind. In any sport, one's intentions can easily be translated through the body's mannerisms.

In fencing, for example, an opponent may reveal their intention to attack by unconsciously wiggling the fingers of their free hand. This may be the product of mounting inner tension as part of the

growing intention to attack. This
represents the moment of decision: do I
retreat or do I attack at the very moment
my opponent reveals his intentions?

This inner tension is found in every
competitive sport and can be thought of
as 'anticipation'. Anticipation can arrive
in many guises -- doubt, stress, anxiety,
just to name a few. Not only is it
important to learn how to read your
opponent's body language, but it may be
of far more value to learn to suppress
your own. Your opponent will always try
to determine your intentions through
body language.

If you can conquer your behavior and
suppress your body language, your
opponent will have nothing to observe.
You can then impose your strategy,
knowing that your adversary will be left
guessing and will not be able to predict
an outcome. This can be thought of as the
ultimate poker face.

"At first, then, exhibit the coyness of a maiden, until the enemy gives you an opening; afterward, emulate the rapidity of a running hare, and it will be too late for the enemy to oppose you."

This would be called 'playing dumb' and reflects a not-so-common form of strategy. As most are driven by aggression, so too is their strategy driven by the need to dominate a given situation. Feigning a degree of incompetence, one that may prompt your opponent into the belief that they possess superior skills, and thus an easy win is at hand. This can lead to carelessness, creating holes in their attack, as well as a false sense of confidence. And, it is this change in your opponent's behavior and mindset that you will exploit. However, this can work only until your adversary discovers that they have been fooled. But, by the time they have become aware of this, it is already too late. You will have used their brashness against them and taken the upper hand.

"Hold out bait to entice the enemy. Feign disorder and crush him."

There are moments during competition when evasion and deceit can take on different meanings. Evasion and sometimes be referred to as a tactical retreat. However, deceit can take many forms. And it is this idea, contained in the quote above by Sun Tzu that I will focus on here.

Of course, your opponent can become overconfident. Why is of no importance. It is the advantage at hand that can lead to a decisive victory. One needs only to present a lure that tempts the opponent and draws them in for the kill. This may be best achieved by creating an opening in one's defense that the opponent can attack. And during the moment when their attack begins, close this opening and strike.

At times, simply dropping the hands momentarily can be deceiving as well. Conversely, bringing the hands up in a sudden defensive posture is an inborn response to danger or threats, and is referred to as the 'startle reflex'. This is often seen as a panicked response from a momentary state of confusion. And, by conditioning ourselves against this response and holding our position, we may be able to confuse the opponent long enough to issue an attack strategy that our opponent does not anticipate. If we can teach ourselves not to react while keeping a clear mind, the chances of a successful attack go up markedly.

"Move only if there is an advantage to be gained".

It makes no sense to execute a strategy when there is no advantage in doing so. The best time to strike may be when your opponent is in retreat. However, this must be done cautiously, as their retreat may be part of a larger plan of attack. Here, it is sometimes best to plan your attack as a defensive strategy and not allow yourself to wander into a trap that takes on the guise of withdrawal.

This is when assessing your opponent becomes most critical. One must keenly observe while anticipating nothing and when your opponent begins their attack you must strike quickly and instinctively. On the other hand, you may choose to withdraw from their attack in order to gain those precious moments needed to formulate a plan of attack.

What this finally comes down to is intention. Much like a game of chess, what you do or how you move depends on what you consider for your plan of attack. You will best be able to form and execute your strategy based on the observations you make of your opponent. If your opponent's behavior provides you with an opportunity to strike, you must certainly take advantage of it. But when your opponent presents no opportunities while making their attack, it will do you no good whatsoever to expend energy on an attack in progress, when moving back slightly to a momentarily safe distance is all that is needed. Thus, the quote above, by Sun Tzu, may have as much to say about conserving and expanding one's energy as the situation demands, as about moving into favorable situations and withdrawing from situations that present no opportunity for success.

"To secure ourselves against defeat lies in our own hands, but the opportunity of defeating the enemy is provided by the enemy himself".

Achieving victory is a conscious decision made by oneself alone. We make this decision by bringing our fullest potential to the game. This includes all our effort, training, experience, and the fire of our desire to win. There is little room for error when one's desire for victory is this strong. This is not to say that we will always play the game. We are human and we will make mistakes. When faced with defeat, we alone must take responsibility. No one can make our mistakes for us.

Let us now look at this from a different perspective. We cannot expect our opponent to willingly give us our victory -- not on a conscious level. But our opponents can provide us with success through their own mistakes. They may repeat their errors, or there may be a flaw in their strategy or timing. They may even experience a leading moment of confusion or overexcitement. In any case, our opponent's errors or even a brief lapse in judgment can mean the difference between victory and defeat, especially during the last few critical moments.

Commentary on the Japanese Art of War

"When you do everything in a normal state of mind, as it is when unoccupied, then everything goes smoothly and easily."

The body possesses its collective muscle memory, and training begins with teaching the body what to do, regardless of one's chosen sport. As the body is trained, so too is the mind taught to react to those situations created by training. In Eastern martial arts or any combat sports, the goal of training is to allow the body to react while the mind lies unoccupied. The result may be called instinct and is the cultivation of this element of our humanness that is the goal of every competitor.

Instinct does not require conscious thought but lies deep within the shadows of our minds. When we train long enough, our instincts are brought to the fore and they allow us to act and react with increasing speed. There is, however, one thing that stands in the way of acting from one's instincts.

In the heat of competition, our conscious mind can analyze and sometimes overanalyze any given situation or any number of possibilities during the game. It is this tendency of the mind to analyze and make sense of events that might slow our reaction time. In other words, thinking too much can be costly. With enough training and discipline, the body will act and react without the individual having to think about what to do. The elements of one's sport have now become an indelible part of the individual. Movement has become instinctive, instantaneous, and fluid. Conscious decisions and judgment have been replaced by flashes of hyper-alert senses and the discovery of one's keen animal nature.

Your instincts will now know what to do before your conscious mind becomes aware of it. You will see the opening in your opponent's attack with a higher degree of clarity. Or, watch the opposing team's strategy unfold and exploit its flaws with greater ease.

Upon the continuation of training and development, you will come to a point where trusting your instincts can often be the key to victory. Does this mean that our instincts will always be correct? Of course not, we will always make mistakes, hopefully learning from them and incorporating them into ourselves as important lessons. Yet, we must never ignore our instincts. They are an asset in competition and will often lead us to victory.

Commentary on Warfighting

"Combat power is a total destructive force we can bring to bear on our enemy at any given time."

It is said that we are more than the sum of our parts. So too, can this be said of the warrior/ competitor. We all bring to the fight all that is us and more -- training, experience, a level of expertise, confidence, skill, and an instinct sharpened by competition. And yet, there is an intangible quality that can never be accurately described. However, we can get a feeling for this idea through the following quote:

"Only warriors with sacred fire in their eyes possess the will to get back on their feet after being knocked down time and time again."

Commentary on
'On the Warriors Path'

Sacred fire. Might this be the inextinguishable human drive -- the immortal core of the warrior's soul? Is it the driving need to continue the fight, even in the face of vastly superior numbers? Yes, it is all of these things and more. As we are each individuals in our own right, this 'sacred fire' must be discovered and maintained by the individual. We all have much to learn about our own inner, sacred fire. And as we learn about this fire, we, in turn, learn about our individuality, for both are intimately intertwined like vines in a jungle. Take one away and we are lost.

These factors taken together represent the totality of what it means to be a warrior. And, it is this totality which we bring to the arena of competition. It is this same set of qualities that we also bring to the way we live. Some might use the phrase 'all or nothing'. And for the warrior, these words can never be anything other than true.

"Intellect without will is worthless. Will without intellect is dangerous."

Of this statement, the last half is likely of more importance than the first, but I shall cover both. The warrior/competitor must be one who possesses both the willingness to learn and the will to achieve victory. Those who learn what is necessary to win, but lack the drive for victory are wasting their time with the goal that will never be pursued. Certainly, commitment is the key to developing a hunger for victory.

On the flip side, one who possesses the thirst to win, but is lacking in training and skill is a liability. They become obsessed with beating the other guy, causing unnecessary injury, and often taunting others. These individuals compare the adrenaline rush of competition to the experience of riding a galloping horse and tend to display the same lack of self-control. What strategic thinking they can muster is often based on aggression, which quite often can only be tempered by discipline and training by repetition. And, it is the trainer's responsibility to draw taught the horses reins, for the benefit of establishing discipline and self-control needed in order to facilitate a calm, disciplined mental state.

"Success depends in large part on the ability to adapt to a constantly changing situation."

In your chosen sport, you may have developed two, maybe three techniques that have consistently worked. However, your opponent has been able to observe you long enough to know that your techniques are very limited. And upon facing this opponent, he can now predict your behavior. Even if you change tactics, he adapts and uses your predictability against you. The question now becomes, 'Can you make this idea work for you?'

As human beings, we are all creatures of habit and prefer a static environment. In the absence of change, life is simply easier to deal with. However, it could be said that the two great constants of the universe are the speed of light and change. From this perspective, we must learn important elements. The first is unpredictability. The second is the human tendency of habit and pattern. These are polar opposites of each other. However, one can make use of the element of unpredictability in order to keep their opponent off guard. As for the element of pattern, one must maintain a certain degree of control so as not to slip into any predictable pattern. And at the same time, observing their opponent for any sign that they may also be falling into a pattern.

With the inexperienced, patterned behavior is nearly certain and can easily be exploited. One only needs to be aware of the instant that any pattern develops. Even the well-trained, experienced competitor is still prone to human nature and can slip into habitual techniques. Should your opponent take on the behavior of being unpredictable, by executing tactics that appear random, bear in mind that there is very little in nature that is truly random. Human behavior is simply not one of them and it is this seemingly chaotic behavior that will eventually evolve into patterns -- no matter how simple or complex. But, until this transformation takes place, one must combat this chaos with focus and a strong, well-ordered defense that can adapt to these changes quickly.

"Accomplish what you need to accomplish and disappear before being discovered."

'From The Ninja Code'

This section is somewhat repetitive of previous chapters, however, the quote above can be considered a variation on previous entries in this book.

As these words can be applied to competition, we can think of them along the lines of strategy. However, with one crucial difference, your adversary will approach you cautiously, reading your behavior and assessing your weaknesses. They are developing a strategy. You must make your attack with such blinding speed your opponent will not have enough time fto ormulate a plan of attack.

We act to gain the upper hand, so too will your opponent's goal be to achieve the same ends. At the same time, moving in and attacking, then getting out as quickly as you made the attack, may very well leave your opponent the impression that your attack is so swift that he simply didn't have time to react. This gives you the additional advantage of intimidation and can be a formidable psychological weapon.

"The best commander attacks when you least skilled is still making plans."

One who is less skilled or new to a given sport will have a tendency to overthink their intentions. They often confuse themselves or consider many strategies in a short period of time. Even a somewhat experienced competitor, lacking in confidence, can be prone to overthinking. They make strategy a complicated matter and confuse themselves between their many plans of attack. They lack instinct and the ability to think quickly on their feet. And, when they are placed in a position where they must defend themselves, their confusion often collides with panic. They simply are unable to think clearly and quickly enough to formulate a workable plan of action and are easily defeated.

The question now becomes, 'How do I recognize this person?' Exploiting this behavior in an opponent is not the issue. Approaching them with an imposing and somewhat chaotic presentation is usually all one needs. However, picking out the one from the many can be like looking for a weak sparrow among a flock of hundreds. You need only learn a few key traits, such as hesitation or trying to carry out at inappropriate moments. Facial expression can often be a reliable method of determining who may be confused over thinking, or who is lacking in self-confidence.

In the end, it will be the competitor who is unable to sufficiently form a plan of action who will suffer defeat. Certainly, it will be easy to take advantage of this situation. But, one must remember that if you adopt a true warrior mentality, you are obligated to assist them in their development as competitors. To achieve victory over one who seems to be overwhelmed with confusion and doubt, only to simply walk away demonstrates a blatant disregard for your fellow competitors who need to learn. You must show them how they were defeated, assisting them in their development of acquiring more challenging skills and clarity of thought. And someday, they will present you with a bona fide challenge that will truly test your skills.

"The one winning the conflict is not the one who is strongest, but the one who knows how to control the opponent emotionally."

As I have previously mentioned, making an attack from an emotional response is detrimental to achieving success. However, one can take advantage of human nature in order to gain the upper hand. Your opponent has the same goal in mind -- to win. But, they are just as prone to acting out of an emotional response. It is here that confidence is not enough, nor is intimidation. Every sport is far more than physical activity -- there is the inner game. One may call it 'head games' or 'manipulation' -- it is all the same thing. You must challenge not only your opponent's skills and experience but also their emotional self-restraint. They wish to keep a clear, focused mind. In achieving victory, it falls to you to take advantage of human nature and destroy this clarity. This can be most easily accomplished through frustration. This can best be thought of as a response to a failed effort when no plan of action seems to work. Facing this dilemma, your opponent will likely stray into acting without formulating a cohesive plan and may become more aggressive as he becomes more desperate.

It is at this point where your opponent begins to display their weakness, leaving openings in their actions that can be exploited. With this development is the time to strike, making your attack as swift as lightning. This emotional response can develop very quickly and once you force it to occur, you must be ready to take advantage of it. In short, opportunities based on this way of thinking are created by intent and never waited on.

Prologue

The development of the warrior mind should never constitute a means to perfection. This is an impossible role to fill. Even the word 'perfect', in human terms, can never be defined. It becomes empty and devoid of any meaning, simply by virtue of the flaws inherent in all of us as members of the human race. The struggle for the warrior mind is exactly that -- a struggle. And it is this struggle that involves growing our instincts on the road to inner strength, as well as personal empowerment. From confronting our emotional turbulence to the unending questions of our determination and commitment, the mind of the warrior never strays into such meaningless, empty ideas as 'perfection' or 'being perfect'.

Additionally, the individual who, by some error in judgment comes to believe in an attainable, personal perfection by way of the warrior mentality has entirely missed the point. They should not abandon their search but take up half the new with the understanding that this path never reaches an end and that the goal of the warrior is the struggle for ongoing development and learning. For when we cease to learn, we cease to truly live, and if the warrior within us withers and dies.

This book is far from a set of written rules or guidelines. Its contents represent a simple way of thinking that one may use to build upon one's character, and change their approach to what lies at the very core of competition. And, in many ways one's approach to living life as well. The perspective should not be seen as containing any significant meaning or set of beliefs. However, this 'way of thinking', while being far from possessing a religious quality, may be seen as something that might bring a degree of definition to one's own life. For rent one's mind is impacted by an idea, change then becomes an eventuality.

Sources

United States Marine Corps
War Fighting -- The U.S. Marine Corps
Book of Strategy
Doubleday, New York, NY 10036
Copyright 1994

Yamamoto Tsunetomo
Hagakure -- The Book of The Samurai
Kodansha International, Ltd.
Tokyo
Copyright 1979

Thomas Cleary
The Japanese Art of War
Shambala Publications, Inc.
Boston, MA 02115
Copyright 1991
Sun Tzu

The Art of War
Dell Publishing
New York, NY 10036
Copyright 1983

Daniele Bolelli
On The Warriors Path
Frog, Ltd.
Berkeley, CA 94712
Copyright 2003